ISBN: 978-0-692-56273-4

DEDICATION

This text is dedicated to those who get it done, with a smile on their face, rain or shine, again and again and again. You are appreciated. Keep Going!

CONTENTS

Something to do while you're waiting

Waiting? Waiting for what? -Really?

Waiting to turn 50?! I'm going to be fifty in another few months. What happened? The last I knew, I was eleven, looking at my cat through a first floor hospital window when my father brought the cat to appease my dismal outlook after being in the hospital for two weeks with an appendicitis. I mean, really, almost *forty years* have passed. In the interim, I have been waiting. Waiting for so many things. I made all kinds of grandiose plans and went about my daily business. And somehow, all of my waiting, patiently, it worked. What worked? No, not any of my plans, so far, not a single one, at least not in exact terms, but somehow, I achieved *more* than my plans. I am successful in business, not my planned business; my family is great, but even more than what I had envisioned; and my energy and infectious positive outlook on life was not even in the picture. I am president of one firm, vice president in another, and an inventor in a third business with seven patents and counting. But, what happened to financial independence before thirty, playing music incredibly well, and driving a sporty expensive car? Well, actually, some of it happened as I envisioned, but not most. What gives? What gives is that I achieved even more than I thought of, but not of such petty things as a car.

Whoever said, "life is what happens while you are busy making plans", was on track. And just like the golden rule of "doing unto others as you would have others do unto you", the "busy making plans" phrase is close, but not quite there. (Regarding the latter, as someone else has probably said, "do unto others as others would have you do unto them" is much more appropriate.) The notion of "making plans" is missing an important nuance. It is all about the waiting. The idea of a "plan" is an action that you *will be* taking, a goal that you *will be* pursuing, you *will be* obtaining, a notion of "I am not there yet but want to be". There is an implied "some time later" that is not present now. Making plans is good and necessary, but the key is how you wait and what you do while you wait. And, importantly, not really thinking about waiting while you're waiting.

What is this all about and who is this little write up for? Well, as you will learn, the process of writing the text is for me, of course, but it is also for you – teenagers, parents, college grads, in college, older, younger… This is not about the what and why of making it from point A to B in life, but is about recognizing the need to have a strategy, thinking about the strategy, and how, ultimately, everything you do is a tactic getting you closer to your goals. But, the twist is that your calculated well-planned actions are probably just something to do while you are waiting for the real actions to take place. Confusing, I know, but read a little further. Maybe you are waiting for a better job, a position that pays more, that allows you more dignity, to more freely express yourself; getting through some very difficult issue with your spouse; when you just need to graduate so you can get on with life; I want to get to heaven, etc… The range of what we wait for is wildly diverse. How about turning fifty years old and not worrying about it but "waiting" my way through it by writing a brief book? Waiting can be useful. For those with a financial bent, as an analogy, sure you can manage your funds every single minute and maybe get lucky to glean great margin, but very few succeed in this way. Time has to pass, seasons have to change, and investments need to mature. Or, the farming analogy: Do not look backward as you plow a field, but look ahead, otherwise the plow rows are poorly laid. And importantly, looking backward and looking immediately in front of the plow wheels both yield poor results.

What provides the best path? Look to the horizon. But, "look to the horizon" and "the power of positive thinking" is not what this is about. It is what you do while you are waiting - waiting between making the investment and gleaning returns, between planting your seed and harvesting the crop, and planning your life and what actually happens. I am going to introduce you to the idea of something to do while you are waiting.

This little text is about identifying and defining what waiting is, why it is important, ideas for waiting, and how to keep track of waiting so you are not slacking instead of waiting. It is not blue sky "imagine yourself sitting beside a gently flowing brook and becoming one with the water ", but about targeted, specific suggestions.

Waiting - Is that a Verb?

While counter intuitive, I think waiting is actually an action verb. What are you doing? "I am waiting". Hey, that doesn't make sense! Absolutely, it does. Lifting a coffee cup, pushing a wheelbarrow, and digging a hole are definitive action verbs. Everyone recognizes these. How about the phrases, driving me crazy, falling in love, and dreaming. Just figures of speech and not verbs? Perhaps, but they allude to the idea that not all actions are the result of bodily movement. At the most basic level, waiting is allowing time to pass, recognizing that it is passing, and that there is a desired outcome at the other side of the elapsing time. By not doing something, or more appropriately, doing something else while you are not doing that other thing, you are absolutely taking action. Maybe, actually, even two actions: waiting and doing simultaneously. Even better.

Why waiting is important - yes, it is important

Okay, I'll admit, the title is misleading. Waiting is not important. Understanding that you are waiting is the key. Certainly, you could be reading this text while you are sitting in a waiting room at the dentist's office and you know, for sure, that you are waiting. The moments in time that you are not doing what you want to be doing are part of waiting. There is a lot to do in the course of a lifetime and you cannot squeeze it all in to defined buckets or moments of time. Your hopes, wants, and needs will rarely arrive to a schedule. That little nine-month bundle of joy, yep, you can be pretty sure, but everything else, forgetaboutit! (New York accent intended). Understanding this reality, really engraining it into your thought, and embracing it will allow you to effectively and, mostly, happily wait. Either you can morosely dillydally and complain and whine and moan while, "I can't get X", "I am not happy with Y", and "I wish I could Z", OR you can make whatever plans you can to try to get X, Y and Z to happen, touch base occasionally to see how you are doing, and be constructive in other ways in the meantime, you know, while you wait.

Is this just another way of coping?

Delving into a little different aspect of Something to Do While You Are Waiting, there is another useful point to discuss. In another page or two, I will lay out what I call a "SoToDo". These Something To Do items have a really useful part to play and it is that these items make incredibly positive coping mechanisms.

Everyone has something in their life that they would rather not have to deal with. Whether it is work related, home related, the environment, politics, whatever, the dissatisfaction and the general desire to avoid the situation is present. So, what do you do about it? You have three choices. You can continue with life as it is and just bear with it and hope that over time something happens. Second, you can try to address the situation, which I think is always the preferable path, but not always possible. And third, you can find mechanisms to cope with the situation, constructively. Some scenarios are situations that you cannot change regardless of how much energy you exert nor can you change your opinion on some subjects any more than you can change someone else's opinion.

So, what to do? It should be obvious by this point that taking path number one, basically pure avoidance, is not what I would consider an option. Just letting things continue to fester and propagate is not a good idea. When I hear people say, "just let it go", I know that is a lot easier said than done, especially if it's something really near and dear to your heart. So, the options really are to try to address the situation or to find effective mechanisms to deal with the reality that you face. I stress finding *effective* mechanisms that allow you to continue your life and to not dwell and focus on those negative issues. Effective, effective, effective, you need something effective! In my experience, the singular most effective mechanism is to develop a great SoToDo. As noted author Peter Drucker says, "the task of leadership is to create an alignment of strengths, making our weaknesses irrelevant." So here, too. You can make your strengths and positive plans so strong that negatives, while still there, are out of focus and more obscured. By implementing very strong SoToDos, you have created a space for your mind to focus on constructive, additive, powerfully beneficial thoughts. Focusing on your SoToDo(s) allows you to forget, at least temporarily push off and out, those things that really tend to get under your skin. You begin to focus on situations and opportunities much bigger and much more interesting than any complaints you may be harboring in your thoughts. "What man by worrying has ever added a day to his life?" And ultimately, you gain an objective view of the situation that, if nothing else, provides a rational understanding of what you are dealing with.

Looking at coping mechanisms, it is important to note that there are many and I am by no means an expert in this subject. It is useful, however, to understand a functioning definition of coping, what it is and what it is not. My definition of coping is finding positive methods to "happily" live and personally thrive while things happen in your life that you do not like, but cannot readily change. Coping is not rolling over and playing dead. Coping is not doing drugs and consuming vast portions of alcohol. And, especially, if you are being physically harmed, or mentally harmed for that matter, there is no definition of coping that is satisfactory - coping is unacceptable- get help, do not cope and do not think that resolving this is a SoToDo! Get out and get help from qualified people. With the definition in hand, it is important, then, to use coping in context.

Coping is necessary. Why? Two things: A) People, B) Magic only works in movies. Regarding A) It may happen occasionally in your life, but it is very rare that you find someone who is basically another you. As result, and there will always be someone in your life that is an anti-you. But, like in every excellent story that you've read there is always an antagonist and it is part of what makes life interesting. You have to look at it that way. Life would be very boring and not nearly as successful if everyone was exactly like me or like you. No two people are equal, and that should be viewed as a good thing. There are people that view life as basically good and there are those who view life as basically sad, bad or indifferent. By bad, I mean that these are the people that seem to always be complaining, glass is half empty or mostly empty already, people. You know them; they may be your spouse, your boss, your coworkers, the delivery person, the sales person, the person who calls you on the phone… The good news, though, is that all of these people are unique and each one is an opportunity to help you do something better in your life - if you are open to doing it. If everyone in the world was an introvert, afraid to talk to other people, and always kept to themselves, we would have far fewer advances that only develop through the excellent results from groups of people getting together and sharing thoughts. But, we need introverts! Imagine a world that was filled with extroverts. In any group gathering, if you have ever taken part in leadership exercises or group thought training programs, when you have multiple people vying for attention or those that want to be the leaders, it is difficult for anything to get accomplished. Human nature drives some to be more competitive and ultimately we are not as successful as we could be if we were more open to communicating with one another (and if we would make way for other people to take the lead when they have a greater strength in an area than we personally do). We need both introverts and extroverts, and in my opinion, we need both in equal measure, just like we need valleys to be able to tell that the tops the mountains are really high.

About B) There have been many times in my life that I wish I could have just had the resolution appear out of thin air. Can't I borrow your magic wand, can't you snap your fingers, click your heels, maybe?... Shazam, problem solved! But, alas, the number of times that has happened are few and far between. Miraculous things have happened, and some things that have happened have been downright amazing, but that it the rare case. You must work toward what you want, approach it physically and mentally with an attitude that you are in this for the long-haul, realizing that achieving the goal does not define you, but that you are understood by the path you tread, the life you lead, and your positive influence on those around you. It's a tall order, but there is no magic wand. SoToDos can be powerful in your life.

One last comment on coping. There are positive mechanisms and negative mechanisms, and there are benefits of each. Yes, there is a benefit even for negative coping mechanisms, but in moderation, of course, and they should be short lived. Negative coping mechanisms do not lead to healthy outcomes. But, sometimes getting to the point of crisis is needed – and only in that moment of crisis can you realize and engage your full focus on seeking and obtaining the solution.

Something To Do While I Was Waiting – an example

All the background thought out of the way, let's set the stage for considering this technique by delving into an example and seeing how this idea plays out in real life. As I noted earlier, at one point, roughly 22 years old, I was sure that I would be wildly financially independent by the time I was thirty. I would be driving a sporty expensive car, have an amazing job, have the envy of my colleagues, would have a beautiful girlfriend (wife idea was not yet there) and I would be helping to get water to sub-Saharan Africa, preferably with some amazing technology that I would develop. Well, that was in my early twenties.

What was the reality? I had an inside sales job for a company earning less than a fifteenth of what it would take to get me near "financially independent", was driving a used Dodge Daytona that my parents bought for me, was engaged and disengaged from a high school sweetheart, and, well, my friends were pretty much in equivalent boats. Certainly no envy there. However, I also kept a slow steady idea of my "actuated air dam system" for reducing drag on cars, still played my guitar, and continued the dream of "making it". On a daily basis, I showed up to work on time, met with friends, pursued a variety of getting from A to B goals, and eventually got married. I had children, earned an MBA and took select jobs that came my way. All the while, I would occasionally fan the embers of the air dam system fire. It was always in the back of my mind. I conducted more testing. Took on a partner. Designed more aerodynamic products, tested more, sighed with frustration, again and again and again, etc., etc., and so on. "The air dam will be my success, catapulting me to the heights of my desires", I thought. And what happened? Zero, zip, nothing. Mountains of time, energy, and focus. No tangible result! Here I am, some thirty years after I first developed the air dam idea and it is not generating revenue, it is not fulfilling my dreams, all this time, waiting, waiting, waiting for it to bear fruit... I cannot believe I waited all this time! But wait. Hold it. What happened? While I was waiting, I did other things. I was waiting for the air dam to become my financial ticket to freedom. What happened, seemingly, is that the air dam has actually been one seriously long "something to do while I was waiting" project. The air dam was not what I was waiting for - it was one of the things I was busy doing while I was actually achieving my goals. It was something I did while I was waiting.

Something did indeed happen while I was waiting. Look back at what I wanted. Sporty car, amazing job, and relevant "acquaintance envy", beautiful wife, and to provide sub-Saharan water. What did I get? Car: I had a top of the line Audi A8l and a super sporty BMW 550i; Amazing Job: a job that allowed me to travel all over the world, take my family on vacations to China, France, England, etc., and create and build new technologies in the medical field, explore my abilities to obtain patents; Acquaintance Envy: many accolades from an array of acquaintances, and globally as well; Beautiful wife: she is lovely; and, Sub-Saharan water, well, while I did not directly provide water to Africa, I have been able to contribute philanthropically far beyond what I thought I would ever be able to do, both financially and of my time. While I was waiting for the air dam system to give me the financial ability to achieve my goals, I actually was achieving them as I went along.

What is learned from this example? A few things, both practical and philosophical. The air dam is just one example of the variety of the "something to do while I am waiting" projects that I have had, but this project ended up serving a particularly useful role. The air dam project forced me into mechanical engineering concepts, building prototypes, dealing with patents, the EPA, and testing facilities, all of which were beyond my skill. And, frankly, I mastered none of them. But, having these experiences enabled me to excel in other unexpected ways and positively impacted the perception of influential others – and bolstered my self-confidence. So, practically, when you are working your way through and thinking about your particular something to do while you are waiting projects, make your projects at least remotely relevant to your life. Remotely means, for example, that if you think you may want to be a great geologist, you may want to get into rock climbing, jewelry making (especially lapidary work), or spelunking. Do things that come naturally, but that are at least in some tangible way close to what you think you ultimately may want to achieve.

Second, as a practical consideration, do not underestimate the power of the passage of time. It works in finances, it works river against rocks, and it works you toward your goals. Slow and steady does not win the race, but having an overall strategy, using the power of time, and staying engaged in life does. Use time to your advantage. "But I don't have time to do x, y, or z". If you are single or married with no kids, sorry, no dice - You DO have time. Trust me, once you have children, you'll know this is true. If you have kids, there is a little slack, a teeny little bit, but you can still achieve a great deal. Use this time! Ten minutes here and there equates to hours and months. You have to do it. Long-term success is in the short-term choices you make. The single biggest catch that I know of is that time does not pass while you are watching TV and is so hugely important that I dedicate a section on TV later. Spending time thinking about what you are doing and going to be doing should be at the top of your immediate to do list and you should revisit it often.

Philosophically, a few themes can be extracted from this example and pulling them out provides a nice segue into an important discussion on distraction. First though, let's think about the philosophical angles. I am more fully introducing the abbreviation "SoToDo" in this section and that, of course, stands for Something To Do (while you are waiting). SoToDos can be different things to different people, but I would like to suggest a few concepts that I think are particularly important. First, as noted above, SoToDos should be remotely related to what you want at the 100,000 foot, whole life overview level. But, what are the characteristics of a good SoToDo? I provide topics and ideas later, but SoToDos can be huge projects or multiple smaller ones, but too many is detrimental. In my case, I had, and still have, two huge SoToDos, and half a dozen smaller ones at any given time. Generally, it seems that when one comes off, I add another in its place. My huge SoToDos are the air dam project and water propulsion cartridge. No need to go into details, but both are multi-year, "I am out of my league", level projects. The smaller ones are publishing my guitar building book, magnetic coffee pack heater (such a cool idea, I think!), glass kiln forming, audio isolator, etc., things that I can achieve. It is important to have a mix of reasonably immediately achievable and those that will take a little longer. Keep in mind that these are things outside of my day job and I am definitely busy. My daily business is no cakewalk. But, right now, as you read this, it is not during working hours. I am likely thinking, dawdling, or penciling ideas on one of these projects. Or, as is really important, I may be with family or friends! What is the value of achieving goals if you cannot share the fruits of your labor with others? I work and sleep and eat and love and get these things done. You can, too.

Another practical aspect is that chipping away at objectives and having SoToDos requiring sequential thought is important. SoToDos can take an inordinate amount of time if you let them, and sometimes, you may just want to buckle down on something. Generally, though, you will find that the bigger projects, which I suggest that you have at least one, will take prolonged sustained effort. So much effort, in fact, that you are forced to break it down into steps or phases that you can chip away at over time. The idea here is about time, after all. Or, I guess more appropriately, constructively passing time. Additionally, a useful byproduct of these bigger projects is that they force you to think sequentially. This needs to be done, then that will happen, or if not, then this or that. After some critical thinking, an overall plan emerges and you are on, or off, close, or far, etc. It does not matter too much as getting there, the journey, is what provides the most significant benefit. And a further note, you cannot simply strive to attain "a goal". Instead, you must strive to attain something bigger, grander, and more difficult because, invariably, we reach our goals, but tend to slide back away from what we just achieved. Shoot past the intended objective and drift back to target – you have to plan to exceed what the target is, set it beyond the actual goal to actually achieve the real goal. The chart below shows this phenomenon. Sometimes, you can hit the goal exactly, but usually, a little overkill ensures success...

Aiming past the objective to drift back to the target...

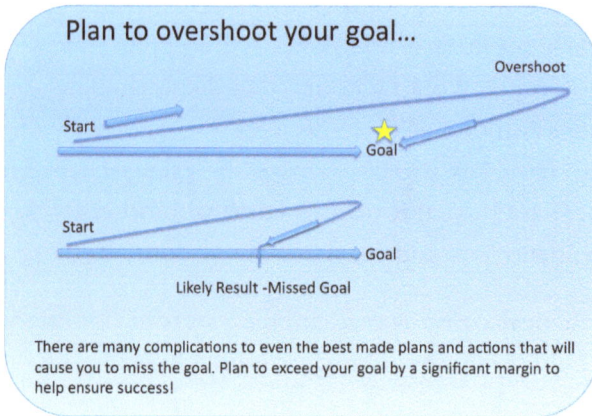

Plan to overshoot your goal...

Overshoot

Start

Goal

Start

Goal

Likely Result -Missed Goal

There are many complications to even the best made plans and actions that will cause you to miss the goal. Plan to exceed your goal by a significant margin to help ensure success!

SoToDos must be more than just action, they must involve thinking, or some may even only be thinking. Einstein said something to the effect that if he had an hour to solve a project, he would spend the first fifty-five minutes thinking about the problem and the last five minutes solving it. Nothing is wrong with action, it is necessary, but more benefit is obtained from really thinking something through than just taking multiple shots at something until you get it right.

Finally, involve others in your SoToDo for maximum gain from what you are doing. Learning by teaching is powerful. What you have learned likely has value and sharing your passion makes contacts that you may learn from or contribute to in the future and it also gathers like-minded people around you. Whether it is business or social, having a network of people that share some part of your interest always makes life more fun while you, and likely your associates, become more successful, happy, and satisfied.

Understanding the general characteristics of SoToDos, and what they entail in terms of required work, might lead you to believe that this is all intended to distract you while you diligently work, seemingly, multiple jobs. This is not the idea. SoToDos are additive to what you are doing, they help what you are doing, and they ultimately result in you doing an overall better job in whatever you do. All of this is achieved while you are not directly focusing on doing a better job. It is not a distraction, it is an attraction - an attraction of knowledge and personal strength within you. Okay, enough philosophy.

Making things

So here is where we start in to the action plans. Finally! Your own SoToDos await you. Or, more likely, you already have some and are going to see them with new eyes –and a refreshed appreciation. You should also figure out some new projects.

To begin, here are some general guidelines. Start with three SoToDos, perhaps three small or one large one and two small. Roughly, or neatly, organize them into a notebook. I prefer paper and suggest using an ink pen that you enjoy. No pencil, though, as there is a temptation to erase things you've done and seeing those "mistakes" is helpful. Plus, redrawing a figure allows you to make it correctly as you see it and I think this is a positive reinforcement of your idea. I also like the spontaneity that paper offers and the ability to quickly scribble off thoughts in the margin. Even the awesome SurfacePro3 does not let me easily do that effectively. Got Paper? For more volume of text, use a computer, but print it out and put it in the notebook. I certainly support "being green", but we are not talking hundreds of pages… As you progress, make notes about what is happening at any given time and what you have discovered, what others are doing (related to your project), add in magazine, email, and search result copies, etc., critical "remember to do X, Y and then Z thoughts and sequences, and especially highlight any light bulb "aha" moments.

When writing, write legibly! I have seen that in the excitement of capturing the moment, I tend to revert to pre-elementary school handwriting. This is bad because the whole idea is to be able to go back and quickly glance over what I was thinking and why it is/was important and poor legibility makes this process get a little muddy and takes too long. (For some background on keeping things simple, where simple is "don't over think it" read "Blink" by Malcom Gladwell.) When you encounter a setback, or better yet when you avoid a setback because you saw it in advance and avoided it, record the details and nuances around what happened and what a better path was or could be. This provides two actions: First, by reviewing the situation and what you did to avoid it or, unfortunately, how you lived through it, you will either feel great that you saw it in advance and you can pat yourself on the back, or as I noted previously, you are taking the better path of positive action, actively addressing the situation, getting it out of your head, and moving on with greater knowledge. It is therapeutic either way. Second, it seems to be in our nature that some lessons are harder to learn than others and sometimes the same problem can arise but look slightly different at first glance. But, by keeping notes on various situations, actions, and outcomes, and being able to quickly peruse them, you will be better prepared to avoid and maximize the situation instead of living through them.

Have defined goals that you can definitively know that you have achieved. "Do better at X" totally does not count. "Talk with my children on the phone at least once a week" counts. There are tons of books on project management, etc., so I will not delve into that realm. The key here is, in SoToDo selection, understand why that particular SoToDo is useful, and ensuring alignment with your 100,000 foot goals.

Consider the time frame for completion. For the large SoToDo, make it tough, but possible. Make it something you can achieve in the next two years, maximum. Once you get going, you should add in a whopper long range SoToDo, but don't start there, wait six months from when you start these first three. Maybe you are an over achiever, start in two months...

Finally, consider your time, talent, and finances. If you will be chipping out time at night, before breakfast, or on your lunch hour, take these time slots into consideration. If your SoToDo involves manual labor, think about when that might that take place. Maybe you will use noisy tools, can only be done in daylight, or during the summer, etc. Regarding talent, I would put this one at the bottom of the consideration list. You can do virtually anything given enough focus and desire. It may take a while to develop a talent, and certainly, using talents that you already have to the maximum effect is great, but this is all about using time and using it wisely. Maybe the time is indeed well spent building a talent that you do not have. Regarding finances, make your SoToDos achievable with the resources you have or can get. If you want to develop a fission power source, assuming you have a degree in advanced physics, you will need access to a lot of money. Maybe you have both, do it! Most of us, however, will need to target more conservative goals at least to start. Work within your means. Again, the whole idea is not to empty your bank account - this is all about something to do while you are waiting!

Working hard, achieving, and balancing enthusiasm is an important aspect. First, just because you have these projects does not mean that you are working multiple simultaneous jobs. It means that you have an underlying continual stream of intent to do something. Once you get into the flow of how this works, it should be smooth and your exertion of effort should be pretty easy. If it feels like you are working way too hard, then you may want to consider creating a new SoToDo, reviewing everything you are doing, and drop the others until you reassess your overall plan. Again, SoToDos are created as additive to your life and ultimate goal achievement and are not intended to become your life. They are to aid you in achieving your overall goals - and you *are* doing it. It should be a little therapeutic to know that you are making small amounts of headway each day and allow you to have a steady flow of ideas, work, planning, review, etc. Once you get established and have a routine, working your SoToDos will seem second nature and very energizing. Sometimes, you do little and you may feel like you are slacking, but these ideas and plans are not for forcing action, but for helping in continuing your overall path forward while you are waiting. Aligning your SoToDo with your life will let you work and, almost, play simultaneously. The second part of this is that you will likely find that you are more energetic than you used to be. To be clear, I mean emotionally energetic, and you have to make sure that you don't go on and on about your SoToDos when someone asks you what you've been up to. You will have a lot more to say, and frankly, most people do not do what you are doing and it will be of some interest to others, but don't burn them out. Leave them wanting for more. In general, I like the statement whoever came up with, "be brief, be bright, be gone". Inside thirty seconds, tell a little bit about the more interesting aspects, and then politely change the focus to the person you are with. (It would be hypocritical if I said I was fully successful in this. I have had to really work on this aspect as I like to talk about projects, but I am learning restraint...)

Small SoToDos

Here is some general information on projects, addressed small and big, and then each is expanded separately. Small SoToDos should be fairly easily accomplished. These can be solo projects that you do completely autonomously and at your own pace and time. They should work with and add on to something you are fairly confident in doing, discussing, leading, or describing and stretch your skills a little or none at all. These are equal parts honing the process and accomplishing the goals. Use these SoToDos to practice the overall concept, make it second nature to write down, plan, review, and extrapolating this to do and not do for the future. You should be able to accomplish any of these projects within six months.

Starting with two or three smaller SoToDos is good. Resist the temptation to add more. Instead, make a list of possible objectives and then prioritize which ones to work on first. Don't worry too much about this task as you will fairly quickly know which ones to work on first. Also, starting with a small number allows you to concentrate a little more. Take your time. You will add in more as you make progress and near the end of any given project. Having a continual stream of small projects is an important tool in achieving your overall goals. Small project reviews should happen perhaps every two weeks or so depending on your definition of "smaller" SoToDo.

Big SoToDos

Big SoToDos should involve needing to interact with other people. There is a great deal to learn and some things you can learn best by watching or talking with other people. Once you become knowledgeable, proficient, passionate, etc., you will likely end up working with others in some way, and your ability to pass on information and skill will reinforce your abilities further.

The projects make you learn something you did not know before, something you do not understand overnight, and maybe something no one else really understands either. They require working through a number of steps, or that you can at least identify some milestones along the way to gauge progress. If you plan and execute these fully, you may find that when you think about what you need to do, your palms sweat a little as you push yourself outside your comfort zone.

These Big SoToDos add to your life, and ideally, add to the life of those around you. If you are going to be miserable and cranky because you are not achieving this "crazy goal" that you have set out to accomplish, forget it. I wrote a book on building an arch top guitar and three quarters of the way through, I came to the realization that building the guitar was great and writing the book was great, but that ultimately, once I had the guitar and book in hand, if I had no one to listen to the music or that would read the book, then, what was the point? I am not saying that you must have a philanthropic bent, but it sure will help. Even if that means that you are trying to increase your personal income, maybe some of that increase ends up in the collection basket on Sunday, in Salvation Army's Santa Clause kettle outside a store, or a donation to the local food pantry.

In the process of thinking this through, you may already have identified that you are in-process on a big SoToDo. That is good. Review it thoroughly, briefly document some history, rethink it, note good things and bad things, what did you think at the outset and what do you think now, where to go from here, etc. Begin your SoToDo in earnest, plan steps from here and proceed.

A big SoToDo should be reviewed every few months, perhaps every four or five months. Too often is not useful, but you do want to understand where you are on the project. On these big ones, just check in occasionally, review notes, and think about next steps.

SoToDo - Waiting as action

The idea presented in this text is not overly complex, but like many things, even though it is common sense, common sense is not so common. No, I am not pessimistic, far from it, but I do often say, "It is hard to think". When we are caught up in daily activities, stresses, time crunches, attitudes, traffic, weather, and business, we sometimes get away from paying attention to the simplest of details. We get lost in pursuing the immediate goal in front of us. We look immediately in front of our wheels and so cannot see the future and we drive a crooked path. So, what follows are suggested smaller SoToDos to prime your thoughts and tactics and then some suggested ideas for searching out your big SoToDo, both generically and as a function of your age.

Identifying some smaller SoToDos:

Let's start with your job. -And no, I don't want to hear it – "I am a homemaker, I don't have a job." Please, you are kidding yourself, of course that is a job. The easiest place to start is to look around. What does your office/living room look like? Do you want to be in that environment? Why, why not, what could be better, what can you change, what should you change, who cares and why, what steps are needed to change, cost, time, and ultimately, what benefit will you gain?

Another possibility: Are you a big picture person or do you love minutia? Your SoToDo should take you into the opposite realm. Big picture people may want to make a SoToDo that requires them to consider one aspect of "the future" for example, and reduce it down to minute details of this, then that, all the way down to what happens at 8 AM on Tuesday. Detail oriented mindsets should take on a SoToDo that entails evaluating and articulating a vision of large scale happenings, megatrends of some pet aspect that they like to fuss over but extrapolated to how that plays out in a bigger setting. For example, say you like rap music and know every artist in the US. Do some research on modern music in Japan, what record music labels are present, what is the culture like, and who is popular, etc. This does not mean that you want to start a label in another country or that you have a bigger goal of pursuing rock star status. What it does do is force you to take your talent for details and apply it to bigger picture scenarios, increases your research skills, makes you more interesting at a party, and shows you that there is a great deal you can figure out and understand if you pay attention.

Get creative: To create is not hard work, it is generally not even work, but it is intentional. Do something fun! Whether it is physical or mental creativity, creation is useful on a dozen levels. Write a brief book, make a video, record a podcast, start a web page (I use SquareSpace), write a blog, play, literally, to your strengths.

Follow your passion. My air dam project started when I was eleven years old and the idea of creating various devices, hardware, in my case, has stuck with me. I am almost fanatically passionate about creating things. At one point, I built a twenty-five foot long 13,000 CFM wind tunnel in my basement to test some aerodynamic ideas I had. Passion? Absolutely, and sharing it, discussing it, nurturing it, lead to my ability to effectively convey my talents to others and ultimately lead to creating another business. This is part of my biggest SoToDo and it is not done yet – I started this thirty nine years ago! Admittedly, I did not recognize it as such at the time. Find something you love and incorporate it into your SoToDo.

This next SoToDo suggestion is a basic one and you may not like it. Just listen before you doubt and say "I'm not doin' that part". Here it is. Ready? No TV. Period. No, I am not kidding. TV is a colossal waste of time. Watch a movie, yes, do it, but not every night. Once you get away from the TV beast and find that you are more interested in your SoToDo work, creativity, thinking, talking, researching, etc., you can reintroduce a little TV, but TV is invasive. Be careful. I know, this sounds like an absurd hard line to take, but some time before you sit down at the TV, note the time. When you are finished, note the time again. What could you have achieved in those two hours? Three hours? Those hours operating the singular most sophisticated computer on the planet – your brain - can yield impressive results! And the second part, like it or not, you must physically exercise, at least a little. Gosh, just lost you, didn't I?

Hopefully not. Simple stretches is a good place to start. You can bend both of these tenets a little, but find a way to incorporate them into a SoToDo. You will not regret it.

One last note on small SoToDos. Remember F.M.U.: Friends, Music, and "Useless Hobbies" are excellent choices. Not everything you do has to be directly helping you achieve some goal. It's great if they are targeted, but simply being active and engaged in life is going to move you toward your goals. Being with people that you enjoy, laughing, singing, whatever, is worth planning into your life. And, I do not believe there is such thing as a useless hobby. Everything you do and think becomes relevant in some way, so do many things, master the ones you want to and dabble in others.

Big SoToDos

The general characteristics of a Big SoToDo were laid out in a previous section, but this part is about how to identify possible projects and then start to zero in on the winner(s). The best place to start is with your pen and notebook in hand. Turn to a blank page, turn the notebook sideways so your page is in landscape, and make the biggest pyramid that will fit on the page. Divide the pyramid into three horizontal sections and write in small letters in the biggest lowest section, "Past". Do the same in the middle section but title it, "Present", and then at the top, title it "Future". See the figure.

LIFE PYRAMID

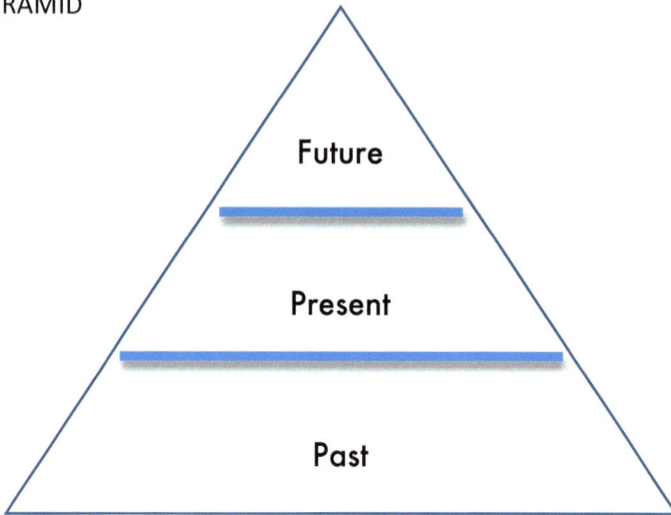

We are going to do a review of your history. The review is strictly of personality traits and various successes and interests that you have had. No negatives. In the "Past" area, write words that would have described you up until roughly three to five years ago, specifically noting various things that you may have done and things that you liked or liked to do. These could include words such as fit, crafty, thought batteries were cool, skier, hot peppers, dreamer, great listener, guitar, elephants, etc. In the "present" section, do the same process, but with today as your frame of reference. In both of these exercises, try to include as many thoughts as possible as we will be distilling them. Don't go crazy with this process. This should take no more than an hour. The farther up the pyramid you go, the more unknowns there are and the more general your input. The pyramid gets bigger as you go down, to the past, as you can fairly clearly see the past and you know detail.

Now stop for a moment. Look at what you *did / how you were* in the past and what you now *do / how you are* in the present and look for similarities. This is useful for trying to understand some of your basic interests so far and what has made it through the years that is part of you. There are likely some items that stand out then and now. If none of them do, don't worry, this is an exercise and is not foolproof. In that case, just try to generalize a general mental picture of then and now and think about how they intersect. Find the common themes, maybe circle them, and then evaluate them. What is contained in these circled areas are some solid candidates to either form the basis of a Big SoToDo or that should at least be a serious consideration for inclusion in one of them.

In the top of the pyramid, "future", list a few concise words of what you hope to be / do / achieve. Put in a few words for things that are easier, some that are harder, and a few that are most difficult to do. If a few words doesn't do it, put in a lot of words. Again, this is just a thought provoking exercise. This is all to help you develop appropriate SoToDos, but virtually anything you do will be fruitful, so move on positively.

Now that you have a few possible targeted ideas, sort through and pull out three "easy" ones or two easy ones and one "harder". Make these your first three SoToDos. The worksheets below show example SoToDos. Reference these worksheets in building your own. A worksheet should form the front cover and guide your overall plan. If something dramatic happens, significantly revising what you will do, make a new worksheet and attach the old sheet to the back after writing one summary sentence across it, "I learned _____". Then move on, it is all good!

The SoToDo Worksheet

Each of the projects that you will develop are totally unique, so much so that I cannot provide much guidance beyond a few examples. But, a relevant aspect is that there are some age specific recommendations that I will make. All of this is based on my experience, my interest in this topic, and success to date. Take it for what you feel it is worth, but these form a solid base from which to progress.

What to do while you are waiting, by age...

What to do while you are waiting to attain 25 years of age. The basic concept, "sorry, it's all up hill". Yep, up hill, both ways, coming and going. I do not want to be in your shoes again. There is so much that you have learned through education and from parental inputs, friends, etc., and you want and expect all that life has to offer. But guess what, you have to work for it, it is not easy work, and the deck is stacked against you. Can you make it? Absolutely, and you can make it exceptionally well at that. In fact, the initiative you have taken to read this far and to be considering this SoToDo planning, means that you have an open mind and willingness to consider another opinion. Try the ideas presented. Make them your own. Tailor them to what you think will work best.

There are a few steps that seem to be most critical at this point. The first thing to start immediately is to start saving money according to a regular schedule – and into something you cannot easily access. You have a huge benefit in long term growth to take advantage of. That is really an easy SoToDo and it forms the basis of the Small SoToDo example below. At this age, developing your repertoire of knowledge and discovering your adult passion takes center stage. I suggest a bevy of Smaller SoToDos stretching you into various areas of interest at first, and then add in two bigger ones after a year or two.

Before you look at each of the following examples, write down a few ideas that may be developing in your thoughts. Scribble your thoughts and come back to them later. These are some of your initial impressions and will likely be some of the best.

Example of small SoToDo

Saving Money

SoToDo Worksheet

Project Summary: Date: __February 27, 1994	Financial Planning, setting a little aside… Starting saving now allows me to compound my money over a long time and helps increase stability in case of large cost appliance, house, car, job…
Rough Time To Complete?	Two business days (+40 years)
When will work be done? (Where and When can I work on this?)	Can do this at home plus need a trip to the bank…
What skill is involved? (Do I have it, need it?)	Consider the available options for automatic investing, how does it work? Input from someone at the bank will be helpful… What are the options? CD's, Mutual Funds, Bonds…
Money? How much and is it worth it?	1) Figure out how much I can allocate; 2) what is my long term savings objective; 3) what is the difference between what the savings will generate and the objective; 4) How and when to close the gap between the two…
Does this align to life "big" goals? How?	With family, need financial stability and flexibility. Private schools, medical, vacations…
Importance – 1 to 10	8 (ultimately a 10, but we are on a good starting foundation)
Specific Goals to achieve	1. Figure out the options? 2. Decide what to do and how much 3. Do it 4. Review in 6 months, add more, less…

	5. Add an annual review date to the calendar
Specific Outcome(s) of achieving the Goal(s):	The outcome of this SoToDo is to have, among other things, a good feeling about the financial stability of my family. Coming up with a concrete plan to work on over the coming years, with milestone objectives, set intervals for review, and reasonable mix of expenses for fun and necessary items is the goal.

My Possible SoToDos?

Example of big SoToDo

Build an electronics repertoire – gear, materials, and a project

SoToDo Worksheet

Project Summary: Date: ___08/10/95_____	Build an electronics repertoire – gear, materials, and a project
Rough Time To Complete?	5 years (due to expense)
When will work be done? (Where and When can I work on this?)	Work will be done during off hours, lunch breaks, and early AM. For soldering and assembly, need an area where small parts can be managed and smell is not offensive
What skill is involved? (Do I have it, need it?)	I know about electronics, but application experience needs to be buffed up. Since I am interested in audio, get a frequency generator, oscilloscope, and learn more about sound physics. Consider stepper motors, too.
Money? How much and is it worth it?	~$2,500. The biggest expenses will be the equipment, but maybe trades can be made and second hand gear is likely to be fine. It is very likely that projects and tasks I develop will need more electronic understanding and these tools will be useful for many years. Get them at the right price when possible, and try to borrow until then.
Does this align to life "big" goals? How?	Going all the way back to 1976, my business "Ricconics" combined Rick and electronics... I am still very interested in electro-mechanical ideas
Importance – 1 to 10	7
Specific Goals to achieve	1. Review projects in the hopper – which ones rely upon these skills to be developed and this equipment to be in hand, prioritize them. 2. Make a trip to Radio Shack, Empire Sound, a

	music store to look at various items they may have. Ask what they would recommend, make a list, estimate costs if new, "do you know anyone looking to sell or trade?" 3. Use the above research and answers and select possible projects, and do one, pick the lowest cost 4. Build an electronic circuit using ICs and Op Amps as they hold a lot of potential across all projects 5. Get stepper, gear, and servo motors and learn how to drive them
Specific Outcome(s) of achieving the Goal(s):	Apply learning to actuated air dam project. Is it real? Does it work? Is it fast enough?
Below for Big SoToDos	**Below for Big SoToDos**
What is the situation?	Work to trade for equipment as money is tight. Components are inexpensive and garage is fine for a simple bench and soldering. Developing this electronic knowledge and ability is key in many future projects, both for personal and professional future.
What actions need to be taken, when, and specific measure of success	What / When / Measure of Success 1. Assessing the gear needed and availability is important. Reading is fine, but hands on experience is a must. Beg, borrow, trade, or purchase gear. Within 6 months 2. Build circuit once until it works. Tear it down and do it again. Complete by August 1996 3. Critically assess what was built. Will it work? Develop a list of why and why not and plan to resolve, complete by December 4. Build a scale system to test full functionality at 60 MPH by August 1997 5. Build a full scale system, shoot video, and investigate patenting...
Why is the order important?	Each step is needed in sequence. Designing a circuit that will work is key, but I cannot design it until I know how! Will everything work as intended? I am worried about the speed of the system. Electronic gear can be rented if need be.

What to avoid?	Don't spend a lot of money to test out the basic concepts. Break up the system into individually test-able pieces and see if it works on a subsection level then combine them as you go.
What trade-offs? Is there a better path? Why /Why Not?	This seems like a pretty reasonable approach. This is a good project to learn more electronics application skill and it is electro-mechanical so it touches many areas so I get the maximum return for the time and money invested
What Other People need to be involved and Plan to include	The library will be important, electronics store staff, maybe the machine shop will let me use the lathe, mill, etc. (building the skill to machine and having equipment could be another SoToDo)

My Possible SoToDos?

What to do age 26 to 50. An appropriate subject line for this age range is that "it's not so steep". In your late twenties, it will be "I'm going to be thirty! Can you believe it?" And at 40, and then all over again at 50, you will have the joy of hearing that you are over the hill, on the downward side, etc. But, the reality is that life doesn't really seem to be a hill but more of a long slope up and then a long slope down. –Does it fit the definition of a hill, well, I guess, but to me a hill connotes that there is a well-defined middle. I don't see it.

In this age range, you have already progressed into an adult, you have had many experiences that you can evaluate and plug into the pyramid, and you can set some solid plans in place. At this age range, developing your adult passions has to be balanced with everything else that is going on, but you have to keep the fires stoked. It is particularly important to pay attention to what you spend your "idle" time doing. If you are single, and there is nothing wrong with being single, you should stay the course, continue to drive a robust mix of smaller and larger SoToDos, and lean on the bigger ones as you get into your late thirties and beyond. If you have a spouse, but no children, take full advantage of this time and harness the power of both of you! You should both have your own SoToDos, but you should have shared SoToDos also. For whatever reason, I have ended up being a father figure in the business organizations I have been in and the issue I hear frequently is that couples do not do things together. Here is your chance. Do it! (And, another note, religious affiliation aside, as a human, I cannot recommend Natural Family Planning enough. It seems very much like a couple focused SoToDo. It does require planning, it brings spouses into agreement and coordination on this important relationship topic.)

If you have a spouse and children, family actions and needs always come first. But, there *is* time. I suggest fewer smaller SoToDos and two bigger ones that you can work on. Try making one or two smaller SoToDos that are family related in some way or that each can play a role in, especially if the kids are older. It is also important throughout this age to keep smaller SoToDos going that keep your thinking fertile – it can be very stress relieving.

Write in a few ideas that may be developing in your thoughts. Scribble your thoughts in the box and come back to them later...

Examples of small SoToDo

Get Fit

SoToDo Worksheet

Project Summary: Date: _____11/12/2008_____	Shed some of those pounds gained during international travel...
Rough Time To Complete?	6 months and on...
When will work be done? (Where and When can I work on this?)	Walk/cycle in neighborhood, Strongsville rec center
What skill is involved? (Do I have it, need it?)	**Just do it**
Money? How much and is it worth it?	$350 if family joins rec, otherwise FREE
Does this align to life "big" goals? How?	I hope to be able to be fit when I retire, so this is a needed short term and long term benefit, start now
Importance – 1 to 10	10
Specific Goals to achieve	1. Walk daily with Paula 2. Bicycle at least once per week, then twice per week starting today 3. Use the home gym machine three days per week for upper body 4. Do 10 sit ups, 10 pushups each day then increase to 20 in one month 5. Figure out what stretches are useful and do them daily – find out which stretches and exercises are good for knee strengthening.
Specific Outcome(s) of achieving the Goal(s):	Overall health and losing some weight – 5 pounds is the initial target. Six months – May 12/16

Example of big SoToDo

Learn about patents, how to patent, and patent something

SoToDo Worksheet

Project Summary: Date: __July 2001_____	Investigate and learn about patents, try to patent something
Rough Time To Complete?	Not sure, but it can take years to obtain a patent from what I have heard, add to that the time to figure out something to patent – air dam is a very likely target
When will work be done? (Where and When can I work on this?)	Can be done anywhere, research needs to be done in library and on the internet
What skill is involved? (Do I have it, need it?)	Creating and technical writing ability I have; how to patent will likely take lawyer input, so work on that aspect
Money? How much and is it worth it?	Expecting $5,000, but not sure, and that does not include development of whatever I will try to patent. This ties in to all of my desired future professional plans and I think it is a very important area to learn and succeed
Does this align to life "big" goals? How?	100%
Importance – 1 to 10	8
Specific Goals to achieve	1. Obtain and read books, articles, etc. on how to patent 2. Critically evaluate the cost and the practical reality of timing 3. Pending learning in 1 and 2, pick one of the Ricconics product ideas and write up as much of patent as possible, find someone that can do CAD work at low

	cost 4. Find a patent lawyer, evaluate costs, and doing as much as possibly on my own, file a patent 5. Obtain a patent
Specific Outcome(s) of achieving the Goal(s):	Patent one of my ideas and while in the patent process, begin to commercialize the product
Below for Big SoToDos	**Below for Big SoToDos**
What is the situation?	Outside of my salary working a day job, I hope to ultimately be able to retire earlier in life than later and this may lead to opportunities to gain increased cash flow and overall income, plus it adds to my marketability and knowledge, bringing value to employers
What actions need to be taken, when, and specific measure of success	What / When / Measure of Success 1. 3 months to read and know, generally, what the scoop is. 2. One year to select the idea and write a patent 3. Within 6 months, find legal counsel and figure out how to pay, what needs to be done, how to do it 4. By July 2003, have submitted a patent 5. Get a patent – perhaps by 2005 (not sure how long it takes, plan to revisit this section
Why is the order important?	This one has to go by the rules, the only exception may be if I find legal that is ridiculously inexpensive, which I do not expect. The other part in this is that it makes sense to patent something real. It may make sense to put more effort into commercializing work than driving a patent too hard without a real product. Revisit this as I go.
What to avoid?	Don't jump at the first lawyer that shows interest. What are all of the costs and how much of my life will I need to spend with this person? Seem trustworthy and not rake me over the coals financially? Will they educate me while "we" do the patent? How are you going to get drawings made? Need good clean CAD models?
What trade-offs? Is there a better path? Why /Why Not?	What if it turns out that the process is so bloody complex that a wrong comma placement makes you resubmit your application, etc.?

What Other People need to be involved and Plan to include	More than anything, I need to keep an eye out for legal counsel. Need a cost effective option with a philanthropic bent to help me without breaking the bank

My Possible SoToDos?

What to do age 51 to 80. Dump the "shoulda, woulda, coulda", and embrace, "hey, this isn't a hill"… When thinking about how to queue up this section, one of my father's axioms came to me. He says, "swing easy, hit the ball hard". This is in terms of golf. The intention is that you do not have to swing with all of your might to get a great shot. Let the club do the work for you and concentrate on form, on finesse, and confidence. This is quite apropos for this age. Part one is that if you haven't been working on SoToDos and have no overarching goal, it is not even remotely too late. Forget any, "I should have been doing x", "I would have Y", and "I could have made Z"… Age is not a hill and you are not over it. Part two, is that this age may be thought of as the antithesis of the "getting to 25" range. At this age, you have a vast accumulation of knowledge and experiences, so much so that you will have to use a finer tipped pen to be able to squeeze all the thoughts into your pyramid. You have a huge advantage. In many respects, you are starting out ahead of the curve. One caution though, and you have to break this one free – you are possibly set in your ways and you need to be open. Don't be afraid to start fresh, do something that you have never even remotely considered, in fact, maybe it is useful to force yourself into a small SoToDo that pushes you out of your comfort zone.

Write in a few ideas that may be developing in your thoughts. Scribble your thoughts in the box and come back to them later…

Examples of small SoToDo

Re-evaluate finances, insurance, retirement

SoToDo Worksheet

Project Summary: Date: ___May 2007_____	Overall finances review
Rough Time To Complete?	3 months
When will work be done? (Where and When can I work on this?)	Gathering documents and laying it all out can be done in the evenings and popping it all into Excel will be useful. Net access is needed to research funds, etc.
What skill is involved? (Do I have it, need it?)	We should be able to do this without a financial advisor, but keep that option open. Find some good retirement planning calculators
Money? How much and is it worth it?	Costs nothing unless we get an advisor involved and that can cost %
Does this align to life "big" goals? How?	100%
Importance – 1 to 10	10
Specific Goals to achieve	1. Gather all financial docs – mutual funds, 401ks, savings, checking, electronic banking history, insurance costs, tax return; will social security exist and be relevant? 2. plug everything in to Excel and chart out where our money goes complete in one month 3. Further evaluate college ideas to finance 4. Use a retirement calculator to estimate savings plan – complete by End of June 5. Reallocate mutual funds, increase/decrease automatic account contributions to achieve "the plan" – and reassess in two years
Specific Outcome(s) of achieving the Goal(s):	Visibility to what we need to do to stay on course and set expectations

Examples of big SoToDo

Right size – what to right-size and priority

SoToDo Worksheet

Project Summary: Date: ____June 2012____	Right sizing our house This is at least a year long project and affects the whole family
Rough Time To Complete?	2 to 3 years
When will work be done? (Where and When can I work on this?)	During evenings and weekends and includes everyone at various times
What skill is involved? (Do I have it, need it?)	We have the skill, but need to continue to promote "the will"
Money? How much and is it worth it?	Actually saves us money and donations can be written off
Does this align to life "big" goals? How?	Yes, less material possession and "things" to deal with we see as good positive life goals
Importance – 1 to 10	8
Specific Goals to achieve	1. Start talking about the idea of moving and begin more aggressively donating – start now 2. Working around kids schedules, and frame of mind willingness, go through accumulated items and get the donation pile growing -1 year 3. Assess college apartment needs and figure out what to keep for that purpose 4. Figure out what to do with my workspace and tools – by fall 2013 (if we sell in Spring 2014 5. Decide when to sell, who to use – around fall 2013 6. Start investigating where to live and what options – condo? Fall 2013
Specific	Downsize belongings and move into something that

Outcome(s) of achieving the Goal(s):	allows less house work, but be inviting and comfortable. Be able to lock the door and go if we want to. Sell, buy, and move in Spring 2014
Below for Big SoToDos	**Below for Big SoToDos**
What is the situation?	We have a lot of stuff – twenty+ years of marriage, two children, hobbies, sports, arts and crafts, etc.,, and the yard is a lot of work, the driveway shoveling, gutters, and leaves and and and… Condo, seems ideal. But, we need everyone to feel okay with what we are doing and how we are doing it, so it takes time and discussion over time. I think everyone is in support, but it can still be emotional. As we age, spend energy on keeping fit, not keeping a house looking good. Paula and I are in total agreement on this topic.
What actions need to be taken, when, and specific measure of success	What / When / Measure of Success 1. The overarching ideas are in the steps above, but get kids to review their items and downsize or condense 2. Rick condense the workspace 3. Donate donate donate 4. get house prepped and looking great – remove wall paper from entire entry area, stairs, etc. – big project 5. Figure out where we want to live, scope out what is available, and plan for Spring 2014
Why is the order important?	We are not in a rush, so plan the work and work the plan. If we do end up selling our house before we can move in somewhere, we want to figure out what to do with as little stuff as possible.
What to avoid?	Don't discard or donate anything that is someone else's as there may be some attachment. This means work around children's schedules
What trade-offs? Is there a better path? Why /Why Not?	Moving can be pretty traumatic and tons of work, so break it up into smaller pieces
What Other People need to be involved and Plan to include	Need realtor, movers, and way to get big items donated (Furniture bank pickup?)

What to do ages 80 to 100+. Motto: Talk, smile, teach, and leave no trace, except good vibes (and maybe some cash!) I like the title of this section. Not that I want to rush it, but I am sort of looking forward to getting to this point. One of my SoToDos is to retire from the business world and get into teaching, perhaps formally, maybe not. (What I'll teach, who knows, but I am pretty sure it will not be writing!) At ages 80 plus, you carry a diverse array of experiences that makes creating SoToDos a breeze, but determining what to focus on may become cloudy. It is my suggestion that you focus outward. Focus on family, friends, and those in need. Make your SoToDos as grandiose as you like, long ranging and short because, hopefully, you are retired and have more time, you've been through the whole "materialism" part of life and realize that you do not care about that so much. A great SoToDo, if you have not already done this, is to right-size you and your spouse's living arrangements. Make a SoToDo of teaching someone a forgotten expertise that you have (like hand churning ice cream or making cheese), be involved in your local chamber of commerce or development board (because wisdom of age and a calm demeanor is certainly needed there) and if the body is only partially willing, find ways to use your mind - edit poor English in brochures from companies in other countries, volunteer for the local telethon, etc. Live to bring joy to yourself and others, make that the SoToDo of your lifetime.

Write in a few ideas that may be developing in your thoughts. Scribble your thoughts in the box and come back to them later…

Examples of small SoToDo

Maintain muscle mass and upper body strength

SoToDo Worksheet

Project Summary: Date: __Whole life__	Maintain muscle mass, upper body strength, and heart health
Rough Time To Complete?	On-going, five days per week minimum
When will work be done? (Where and When can I work on this?)	At home, Park, Recreation Center, any time of day (but not too close to going to sleep)
What skill is involved? (Do I have it, need it?)	Generally speaking, my overall physical condition is good, but heart health and maintaining strength require continual effort
Money? How much and is it worth it?	Free if at home, recreational center may be $300 to $500 per year
Does this align to life "big" goals? How?	100%! Being able to enjoy life now and in retirement requires energy. Heart health is, of course, a critical requirement, but for great quantity and quality of life, being able to move, go place to place, and explore through travel, physical strength and capability are required.
Importance – 1 to 10	10
Specific Goals to achieve	1. 10/25 – 10,000 steps per day – everyday, Body Mass Index 25 or less 2. Do 20 pushups every day 3. Do 20 sit-ups every day 4. At least 20 minutes of accelerated walking / jogging/ or combination five days per week, on treadmill, rec center, or shopping area in colder temperatures 5. If possible, add in swimming laps as it helps develop

	good lung capacity, muscle tone, and stamina 6. Learn Tai Chi or some Qi Gong to help motor control and the critical need for physical and mental balance
Specific Outcome(s) of achieving the Goal(s):	Maintaining overall health is the goal, not bulking up, running a marathon, or swimming the English Channel...

My Possible SoToDos?

Examples of big SoToDo

Make a year long plan to help a struggling charity prosper, finances, labor, logistics

SoToDo Worksheet

Project Summary: Date: ____75 Years Old___	Help a charity prosper, improve finances, better coordinate labor, manage operational issues and logistics, get creative
Rough Time To Complete?	2 to 5 Years
When will work be done? (Where and When can I work on this?)	Depending on the charity, much of the work will be done working with the charity staff at the locations where they do their work. I also envision, however, that much work involved can be done at home or the coffee shop as it involved creating, brainstorming, and envisioning what, why, how, etc., to achieve the aims of the charity.
What skill is involved? (Do I have it, need it?)	Having already spent thirty years in business building domestic and internationally successful organizations, motivating personnel, creatively marketing ideas and products, strategizing, managing profit and loss, etc., the skills are likely there to be helpful. Learning the specific nuances of the charity is a good project and forces continued life-long learning to help stay mentally sharp.
Money? How much and is it worth it?	Low or no cost, definitely worth it
Does this align to life "big" goals? How?	In the biggest picture, "Help others achieve and thrive, not just survive" is a worthy goal!
Importance – 1 to 10	10
Specific Goals to achieve	1. Find a charity or other non-profit (or maybe even for profit) that I want to help and that I may benefit

	2. Evaluate them from the outside looking in 3. Develop an estimated "how I can help" 4. Talk with them and determine a path 5. Do it
Specific Outcome(s) of achieving the Goal(s):	Greater success for the charity according to its own standards of success
Below for Big SoToDos	**Below for Big SoToDos**
What is the situation?	This will depend on the charity and, to some extent, my physical abilities
What actions need to be taken, when, and specific measure of success	What / When / Measure of Success 1. What charities are nearby? What do they do? Determine, from the outside looking in, do they look healthy? Does it look like they need help? Importantly, do I know anyone associated with the charity that may help me establish rapport? Tread softly. 2. Develop a brief but powerful summary, maybe one page, saying what the issue is, how I can help, and what qualifications make me think so. 3. Communicate with the charity and get involved – if they do not want your help, start over elsewhere… 4. Take time to understand and fully evaluate what is going on inside and outside the charity. Compare it to what I saw from the outside looking in. Do they match? Why and why not (do both aspects as it helps identify what makes them who they are or who they want to be). Summarize the findings and put it into concise words to be the guiding premise as time progresses. 5. Follow the Plan, Do, Check, Act, an repeat method to attain goals (Reference any quality book or web search the method)
Why is the order important?	Before approaching a group, especially a non-profit, it is important to understand that, as stereotype, these are passionate people. Do not offend them by even remotely assessing that I know more than they do. Do homework to define facts before doing anything.
What to avoid?	I want to help, not become the principal driver
What trade-offs? Is there a better	This is a good use of time provided balance is maintained

path? Why /Why Not?	
What Other People need to be involved and Plan to include	Ideally, I know someone associated with the group to act as an introductory point, but in the even bigger scenario, I hope to offer guidance, ideas, strategies, and action plans, but it is for the benefit and action taking of people in the group and those they serve.

My Possible SoToDos?

Now that you have read this through, I am confident and hopeful that all of this will seem to make some practical sense. Employ it to its fullest benefit! The process of writing the text was, indeed, for me as one of my SoToDos, but I think you can see how it is definitely also for you. As I noted in the introduction, this is not about the what and why of making it from point A to B in life, but is about recognizing the need to have a strategy, thinking about the strategy, and how, ultimately, everything you do is a tactic getting you closer to your goals. There is an entire philosophical aspect that awaits yet another SoToDo text writing exercise that may come later, but think about that aspect as you delve into projects. Attitude and perception are some of the most powerful tools that you have to work with – and they are free, unlimited, and empowering.

The key take away is that your calculated actions are probably, mostly, principally, etc... just something to do while you are waiting for the real actions to take place, so make them fun, engage others, and be a positive addition to your long term goals. Be inspired to go about identifying and acting on your own personal Something To Do While You Are Waiting projects. Waiting effectively is important and may help bring you and everyone around you a more fulfilling life!

The following worksheets are to be used to help you develop your own SoToDos. They may be a perfect fit, they may not, but they do form a solid base. Tailor them to your own needs and make them work for you.

SoToDo Worksheet

Project Summary: **Date: _____**	
Rough Time To Complete?	
When will work be done? (Where and When can I work on this?)	
What skill is involved? (Do I have it, need it?)	
Money? How much and is it worth it?	
Does this align to life "big" goals? How?	
Importance – 1 to 10	
Specific Goals to achieve	1. 2. 3. 4. 5.
Specific Outcome(s) of achieving the Goal(s):	

Below for Big SoToDos	**Below for Big SoToDos**
What is the situation?	
What actions need to be taken, when, and specific measure of success	**What / When / Measure of Success** 1. 2. 3. 4. 5.
Why is the order important?	
What to avoid?	
What trade-offs? Is there a better path? Why /Why Not?	
What Other People need to be involved and Plan to include	

Draw sketches, diagrams, and ideas here

SoToDo Review

What is happening?	
What has been discovered is...	
The "AHA" moment / thought is:	
Other people are:	
The mistakes I made were:	
Remember to:	

Follow up again on _____

Finished?: _____!

ABOUT THE AUTHOR

(The guy's got a CPA. No, not accounting, but a Compellingly Positive Attitude...)

With a passion for innovation, Rick is continuously working on products, people, and processes. Whether maximizing margin on a business platform in China, optimizing proforma financials for strategic investment, or patenting a technology in magnetic induction heating, Rick is energetically engaged and spreading his "we can do this" enthusiasm.

As a compellingly positive achiever, his work has enabled global corporate success. Accelerating revenue generation through product innovation and portfolio expansion, his skill in effectively managing cross-functional teams and generating and maintaining corporate enthusiasm to attain goals is a hallmark. The brevity of this book on so beneficial a life strategy is a good reflection of Rick's style.

Author of ten patents, multiple texts, and actively engaged in three companies, there are few people with the energy and ability to maintain Rick's constant productivity - and smile.

-Jerry

www.ingramcontent.com/pod-product-compliance
Lightning Source LLC
LaVergne TN
LVHW010028070426
835513LV00001B/21